The Let's Talk Library™

Let's Talk About Epilepsy

Melanie Apel Gordon

The Rosen Publishing Group's
PowerKids Press™
New York

To Aunty Seemore (Joy Moskovitz), with love and prayers for healing. Love, Melanie

Published in 2000 by The Rosen Publishing Group, Inc.
29 East 21st Street, New York, NY 10010

First Edition

Book design: Erin McKenna

Photo Credits and Photo Illustrations: pp. 4, 15, 19 by Les Mills; pp. 7, 20 by Seth Dinnerman; p. 8 © SIU/Custom Medical; p. 11 © John Bavosi, Science Photo Library/Custom Medical; p. 16 © B. Kramer/ Custom Medical.

Gordon, Melanie Apel.
    Let's talk about epilepsy / by Melanie Apel Gordon.
        p.   cm.— (The let's talk library)
    Includes index.
    Summary: Explains the nature, causes, symptoms, and treatment of epilepsy.
    ISBN 0-8239-5414-5
    1. Epilepsy—Juvenile literature. [1. Epilepsy. 2. Diseases.] I. Title. II. Series.
RC372.2.G67 1998
616.8'53—dc21   98-39850
                                                                                                                     CIP
                                                                                                                      AC

Manufactured in the United States of America

Contents

Gabriel

Something is happening to Gabriel. He is lying on the floor shaking. His arms and legs are moving, and he is drooling. Jamie calls Gabriel's name, but Gabriel doesn't answer. His mom moves some chairs out of his way so that he doesn't get hurt. A few minutes later Gabriel calms down. He sits up and looks around. He feels tired and confused. Gabriel doesn't remember what just happened. "You had a **seizure**, Gabriel," his mom tells him. Gabriel has **epilepsy**.

◀ After a seizure, a person with epilepsy may need some comforting.

A Message from Your Brain

No matter what you are doing, your brain is always at work. Your brain cells use electrical signals called **impulses** to send messages to one another. These messages tell your body to do many things such as walk, talk, move, and breathe. Normally, your brain cells send about 80 messages every second. Your brain cells are sending these messages all the time. The messages are sent in a neat and orderly way. You don't even know that they are being sent.

Many organized messages from your brain allow your body to run, jump, and even in-line skate. ▶

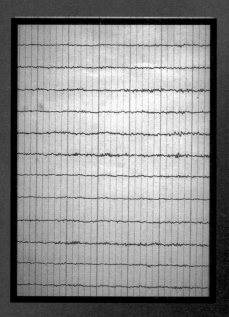

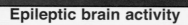

Epileptic brain activity

Normal brain activity

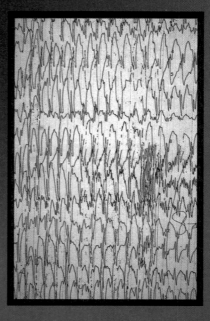

What Is Epilepsy?

Epilepsy is a brain disorder that causes a person to have seizures. If you have epilepsy, some of your brain cells are damaged. Sometimes these damaged brain cells send too many messages at one time. Your brain can't handle that many messages at once. When a message overload happens, you have a seizure. During a seizure, the damaged brain cells send about 500 messages every second. When you have a seizure, you cannot control what is happening with your body.

◀ The top picture shows normal brain activity. The bottom picture shows brain activity during a seizure. Do you see how the top picture looks much calmer?

Different Kinds of Seizures

All seizures occur in the brain. There are different kinds of seizures. A **generalized seizure** affects the whole body. In this kind of seizure a person becomes **unconscious**, falls down, and has **convulsions**. If a person has a **partial seizure**, only part of the body is affected. This can be a change in the sense of smell, or the person may feel dizzy. The smallest seizure is called an **absence seizure**. A person may just seem "out of it" for a moment.

Even though a seizure may affect your whole body, it occurs in your brain. ▶

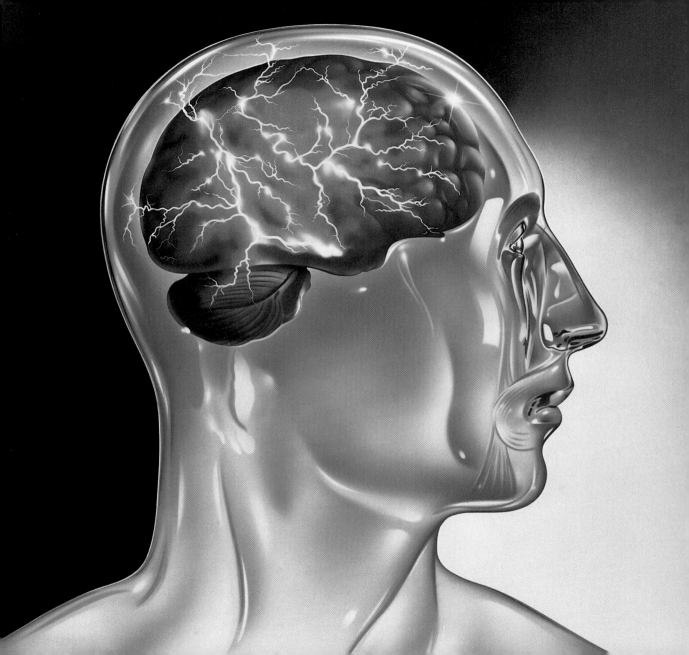

Who Has Epilepsy?

Anybody can have epilepsy. Doctors don't always know why a person gets epilepsy, but about half of the people who have epilepsy got it in one of these ways: a serious head **injury**, lead poisoning, or a very bad **infection** in the brain. When a person's brain cells get damaged, he or she could get epilepsy. You can't tell if a person has epilepsy just by looking at him. And you can't catch epilepsy from someone who has it.

◄ Kids with epilepsy can do the things they enjoy, just like kids without epilepsy.

What to Do When Someone Has a Seizure

If you see someone having a seizure, there are some things that you can do to help. First, move objects out of the way so that the person doesn't knock into them. If you can, put something soft under her head. If there is a grown-up nearby, ask him or her to turn the epileptic person on her side so that she doesn't choke on her **saliva**. And don't hold the epileptic person down or try to keep her body still. When the seizure is over, you can help the person relax and feel comfortable.

Seeing someone have a seizure can be scary. Try to stay calm and help that person after the seizure is over. ▶

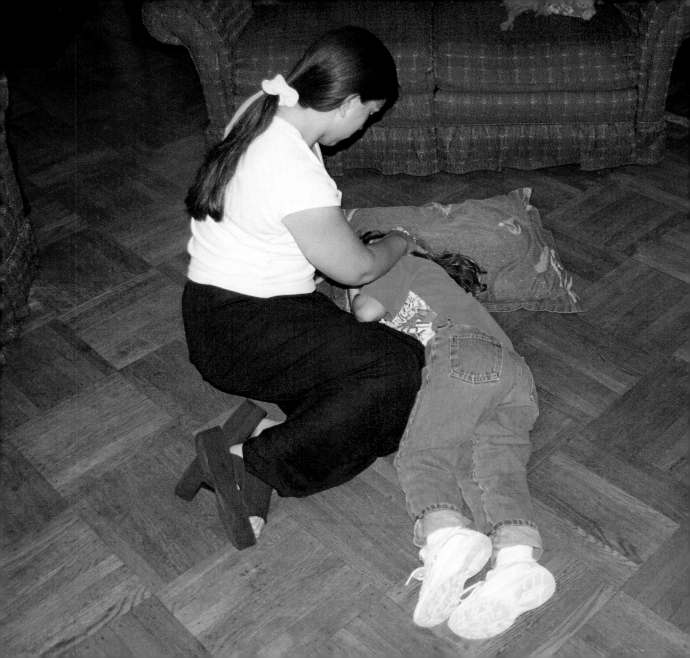

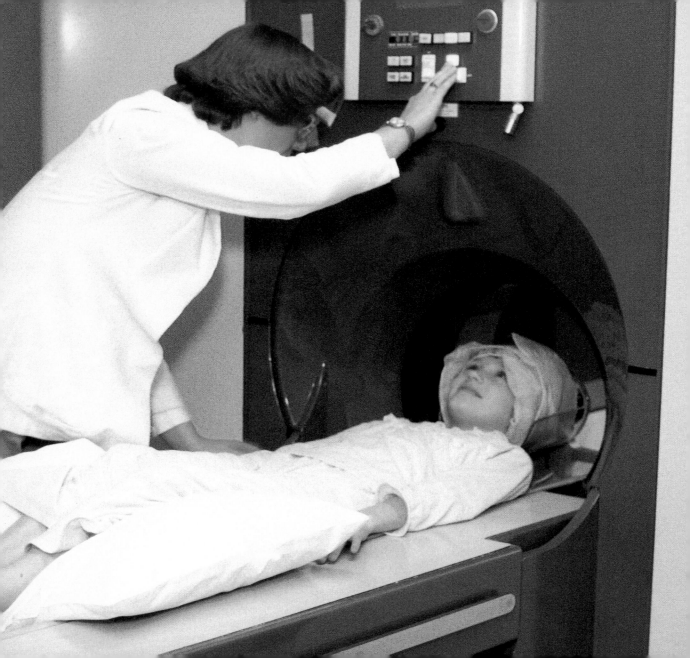

Seeing the Doctor

If you have had seizures, your doctor will talk to you about them. She will ask you questions. She will do some tests to see why you are having seizures. An EEG shows **abnormal** activity in your brain that might be causing seizures. A CAT scan is a 3-D X ray of your brain. An MRI can also help doctors see what is happening in your brain. Both a CAT scan and an MRI let doctors see your brain. None of these tests hurts at all.

◀ Ask your doctor or nurse all the questions you want before a CAT scan. That way you'll know what to expect.

Treatment

There is no cure for epilepsy. But there are many different medicines that can help control seizures. For most people who have epilepsy, **anti-seizure** medicine keeps them from having seizures. Some people who have epilepsy take one anti-seizure medicine. Others may need to take two or more medicines to control their seizures. But for some people the medicine controls only some of the seizures. If the medicine doesn't control the seizures at all, the person may need **surgery**.

By taking her medicine regularly, someone with epilepsy can control her seizures. ▶

Side Effects of Medicine

When your doctor gives you anti-seizure medicine you must follow directions and take it every day. Until you get used to the medicine you may feel some side effects. You might feel tired, cranky, or **nauseated**. You may get a rash. You might even have more seizures than you had before. The doctor may have to change your medicine a few times to find the one that's just right for your body. But once the right medicine is found, you should feel much better.

◀ Make sure you tell your doctor if your medicine makes you feel sick. He will do his best to help you feel better.

Things to Remember About Epilepsy

If you have epilepsy it is important to do things to keep from having seizures. You should always take your medicine on time and get enough sleep. Visit your doctor regularly and always tell her how you are doing. Remember that having epilepsy is nothing to be embarrassed about. If you take good care of yourself, you can keep your epilepsy under control and live a very healthy life.

Glossary

abnormal (ab-NOR-mul) Out of the ordinary.

absence seizure (AB-sents SEE-zher) A type of seizure when a person seems "out of it" for a moment.

anti-seizure (AN-ty SEE-zher) Something that prevents a seizure from happening.

convulsion (kun-VUL-shun) Uncontrolled, violent shaking.

epilepsy (EH-puh-lep-see) A brain disorder that causes seizures.

generalized seizure (JEH-nuh-ruh-lyzd SEE-zher) A seizure that affects the whole body.

impulse (IM-puls) An electrical signal that brain cells use to send messages to one another.

infection (in-FEK-shun) A disease caused by germs.

injury (IN-juh-ree) Physical harm or damage done to a person.

nauseated (NAW-zee-ayt-ed) Feeling sick to your stomach.

partial seizure (PAR-shul SEE-zher) A seizure that affects only part of your body.

saliva (suh-LYE-vuh) The liquid in your mouth.

seizure (SEE-zher) A sudden burst of extra brain messages that causes abnormal brain activity and can cause abnormal body movement.

surgery (SER-juh-ree) An operation.

unconscious (un-KAHN-shus) Not aware of what is going on.

Index